This book is not about study skills.

It's about getting a good job after you graduate.

Most students' #1 reason for attending college is 'to get a good job'.

The skills outlined in *Making Your Mark* will help you graduate from college. But more importantly, these skills will help you become employable. It's kind of like a 2-for-1 deal. As you develop your college success skills, you'll actually be developing the qualities that employers look for: good work habits, time management skills, and an organized approach to getting your work done at a high standard. If you approach your college years as professional development for your career, you'll be well prepared for the workplace, and you'll come as close as you can to guaranteeing yourself a good job upon graduation.

LDF PUBLISHING INC

P.O. Box 45, Port Perry, ON Canada, L9L 1A2 Tel: (905) 985-9990 Fax: (905) 985-0713 Email: ldf@sympatico.ca
www.ldfpublishing.com

Acadia University Adelphi University Alamo Community College Alfred State College Algonquin College Alice Lloyd College Alleghany College Alleghany College of Maryland Andover College Angelo State University Appalachian Bible College Aquinas College Asheville-Buncombe Technical College Assumption College Athens Area Technical College Atlantic Bible College Atlantic Union College Assiniboine College Auburn University Ayers State Technical College Azusa Pacific University Baker College at Flint Baker College at MountClements Barton College Beaufort County College Belleville Area College Bethune-Cookman College Bluefield College Bohecker Business College Bowling Green State University Bradford School Bridgton Academy Briercrest College British Columbia Institute of Technology Brescia College Bucks County Community College Buffalo State College Butler County Community College Cabot College California Academy of Merchandising Art & Design California Christian College Carlow College Camden County College Camosun College Caldwell College Canadian Plastics Training Centre Canadian School of Natural Nutrition Canadore College Carl Albert State College Carleton RC School Board Cégep de Baie-Comeau Cégep Beauce-Appalaches Cégep de Chicoutimi Cégep de la Gaspésie Cégep Joliette-de-Lanaudière Cégep de Jonquière Cégep de St-Félicien Cégep Rimouski Cégep de Saint-Foy Cégep Saint-Jean-sur-Richelieu Cégep de Sept-Iles Cégep de Trois-Rivières Centre de Formation Champlain Centennial College Central Arizona College Central College Central Christian College Central Newfoundland College Central Ohio Technical College Central Texas College Central Washington University Champlain College Champlain Regional College Charleston Southern University City College of San Francisco Clarendon College Clarion County Career Center Clarion University Clark University Clarkson College Cleveland Chiropractic College Clinch Valley College Coastal Carolina University Coker College Collège de l'Assomption Collège Cambrian Collège Communautaire de Nouveau- Brunswick College of Geographic Sciences Collège de l'Outaouais Collège de Saint-Boniface Collège Merici College of Mount Saint Joseph College of New Caledonia College of New Rochelle Collège Northern College of Notre Dame College of St. Francis College of Saint Elizabeth College of the Albemarle Colorado State University Columbia College C olumbia Bible College Community College of Philadelphia Community College of Rhode Island Computer Training Academy Concord College Concord Community College ConCorde Career Institute Corning Communiity College Concordia College Concordia University Conestoga College Confederation College Coop du Collège de la Région de l'Amianté Coop Scolaire Notre-Dame Corning Community College Criswell College Cuesta College CUNY - Kingsborough Curtin University of Technology Cuyahoga Community College Dakota State University Dalhousie University Dane County Private Industry Council Danville Area Community College Darton College Dawson College Del Mar College Delaware Technical College Delaware Valley College Delgado Community College Dodge City Community College Dordt College Douglas College Douglas MacArthur State College Duluth Business University Durham College Dyersburg State College East Coast Bible College East Kootenay College East Tennessee State University Eastern College Eastern Maine Technical College Eastern New Mexico University Eastern Oregon State College Eight Northern Pueblos Council Emily Carr College Emmanuel Bible College ETI Technical College Everett Community College Fairview College Fanshawe College Fashion Careers of California College Faulkner University Feather River Community College Finger Lakes Community College Fisk University Fitchburg State College Fleming College Florida Institute of Technology Florida Metropolitan University Fontbonne College Fort Peck Community College Franklin College of Indiana Fraser Valley College Frostburg State University Gadsden Community College Gallipolis Career College Gateway Community College George Brown College George Fox University Georgia Perimeter School Georgian College Glendale Community College Glenforest Secondary Gogebic Community College Golden State Business College Gonzaga University Grace College Grande Prairie College Grant MacEwan College Griggs University Guildford Technical Community College Hagerstown Business College Harold Washington College Hartwick College Hawaii Community College Hazard College Heald Institute of Technology Hesser College Hinds Community College Hocking College Holland College Holy Family College Horry Georgetown Technical College Howard Community College Howard Payne University Howard University Horry-Georgetown Technical College Humber College Humphreys College Huntington College Illinois Eastern College Indiana State University Indigo Books Institute of Design & Construction Institut de Technologie Agroalimentaire Interstate Career College Iona College Iowa State University Iowa Western University Itasca Community College Jamestown Business College Jewish Hospital College of Nursing John M. Patterson State College John Tyler Community College Johnson Technical Institute Jones College Juniate College Kankakee Community College Kaskaskia College Keewatin Community College Kennebec Valley Technical College Kettering College of Medical Arts Keyin Technical College Kings River Community College Kirksville College of Osteopathic Medicine Kwantlen College La Cité Collégiale Labette Community College Labrador College Lake Sumter Community College Lakehead University Lakeland College Lamar Community College Lambton-Kent School Board Lancaster Bible College Lander University Langley School District Laurel Business Institute Lawson State Community College Lees College LeHigh Carbon Community College Lemar University at Orange Lethbridge Community College Lewis & Clark Community College LIFE Bible College Lincoln Technical Institute Lincoln Land Community College Lincoln University Loch Haven University Long Island University Longview Community College Lorain County Community College Louisiana State University Louisiana Technical College Lowell Middlesex Community College Loyola College Lubbock Christian College Madisonville Community College Malaspina College Mankato State University Maui Community College McHenry County College McMaster University McMurry University Madison Area Community College Manchester Community College Marianopolis College Medicine Hat College Mesabi Range College Miami University Michigan Christian College Michigan State University Middle Georgia College Middlebury College Middlesex Technical College Midland Lutheran College Midlands Technical College Midway College Milligan College Mission College Mississippi County Community College Mohawk College Mohegan College Montana State University Montclair State University Montgomery College Morehouse College Morningside College Mount Carmel Health System Mount Saint Vincent University Mount San Jacinto College Mount Wachusett Community College Multnomah Bible College Murray State University Napa Valley College Nash Community College Nassau Community College National School of Technology New Brunswick Community College New England Institute of Technology New Hampshire Technical College New Mexico State University Niagara College Niagara County Community College North Carolina A&T State University North Greenville College North Harris College North Island College North Park College North Park Secondary Northern Alberta Institute of Technology Northern College Northern Marianas College Northern Michigan University Northumberland Board of Education Northwest College Northwest College of Art Northwest Tennessee E.D. Council Northwestern College Northwestern Michigan College Nossi College of Art Nova Scotia Agricultural College Nova Scotia Community College Nyack College Oak Hills Bible College Oakland City University Oakland University Oakton Community College Odessa College Ohio Business College Ohio Institute of Photo&Design Ohio Northern University Okanagan University Oklahoma State University Olds College Olean Business Institute Ontario Hockey League Otero Junior College Otis College of Art & Design Owensborough Community College Ozark Technical Community College Pacific University Palau Community College Palmer College of Chiropractic Parkland Regional College Pembroke State University Penn Commercial Inc Penn State University Pennsylvania Institute of Technology Pensacola Junior College Philadelphia College Philadelphia Institute of Culinary Arts Phillips County Community College Pikeville College Pittsburgh Technical Institute Polyvalente Roland Pépin Pope John XXIII National Seminary Porterville College Potomac State College Provo College Quincy University Quinebaug Valley College Rancho Santiago Community College Randoph-Macon Women's College Rapid City Area Schools Red Deer College Red River College Redeemer College Redlands Community College Rich Mountain College Richard J. Daley College Rochester Institute of Technology Rocky Mountain College of Art and Design Royal Military College Saint Anselm College Saint Cloud Technical College Saint Martin's College San Diego State University San Juan College Santa Ana College Santa Clara University Santa Rosa Junior College Saskatchewan Indian Federated College Savannah College of Art&Design Sawyer School Schenectady County College Selkirk College Seneca College Seton Hall University Shawnee State University Shelby State Community College Shenandoah University SIAST - Kelsey Institute Sierra Nevada College Silicon Valley College Simmons Institute of Funeral Service, Inc. Sinclair Community College Sir Sandford Fleming College Sonoma State University South Dakota School of Mines and Technology South Hills Business College South Puget Sound Community College Southeast Regional College Southeastern Louisiana University Southern Illinois University Southern Nazarene University Southern State Community College Southern West Virginia College Southwest Acupuncture College Southwest Texas State University Southwest Virginia Community College Southwestern Community College Spalding University Sparks State Technical College Spartan School of Aeronautics Spartanburg Methodist College Spartanburg Technical College Spring Arbor College St. Clair College St. Elizabeth College of Nursing St. John Fisher College St. Joseph's Hospital Health Center St. Louis Community College St. Mary's University St. Meinrad College Stanly College State University of West Georgia Sterling College Stevens-Henager College of Business SUNY - Brockport Suomi College Surry Community College Sweet Briar College Syracuse University Tarleton State University Tarrant County Junior College Taylor Business Institute Taylor University Texas A&M University Texas Technical Health Sciences Center Tiffin University Timiskaming Board of Education Trafalgar Castle School Tri State Business Institute Trident Technical College Trinidad State Junior College Trinity Western University Trocaire College Union College University of Arizona Université de Québec University College of Cape Breton University of British Columbia University of Calgary University of Charleston University of Cincinnati University of Hawaii University of Idaho University of La Verne University of Maine University of Manitoba University of New Mexico University of New Orleans University of North Carolina University of Northern Colorado University of Rochester University of South Carolina University of South Colorado University of Tennessee University of Texas University of Virginia University of Waterloo University of Wisconsin Universitiy of Wyoming Valdosta Technical Institute Vancouver Community College Vanier College Virginia Commonwealth University Virginia Military Institute Virginia Technical Institute Virginia Western Community College Viterbo College Wabash Valley College Warner Pacific College Washington County Technical College Waycross College Wayne State University Weber State University Webb Institute Webster University Wesley College West Tennessee Business College West Valley College West Virginia University Western Illinois University Westmont College Westviking College Wheeling Jesuit College Wichita State University Wilkes University William Paterson College William Penn College Winona Technical College Wittenburg University Wright State University Xavier University York Technical Institute Yosemite Community College District Yukon College

More than 350,000 students have used *Making Your Mark* to get through college.

At over 750 educational institutions across North America.

making *your* mark

5th Edition

Lisa Fraser

Career Directions

24 Time Management Tips

How to Prepare for Exams

Papers, Reports and Assignments

39 Study Hints and Shortcuts

Notetaking Tips

33 College Survival Skills

"We are what we repeatedly do.
Excellence, then, is not an act, but a habit."
- Aristotle

Making Your Mark
5th Edition
Lisa Fraser
ISBN 0-9696427-6-8

Reprinted 2000
Copyright © 1996 by LDF Publishing Inc.
(First published in 1992)

<u>Publishing and Purchasing Information</u>

Making Your Mark can be purchased at special volume disounts. It is also available in French and in software format.

LDF Publishing Inc.
P.O. Box 45, Port Perry, ON Canada L9L 1A2
Tel: (905) 985-9990 Fax: (905) 985-0713   Email: ldf@sympatico.ca
Web Site: www.ldfpublishing.com

Printed in Canada by Maracle Press Ltd.

table *of* contents

new *beginnings* 1

This book is designed to help you get the most out of college, and more importantly, to help you get through college. Whether you're a first year student, a returning student, a student athlete, a student preparing for post-secondary education, or a non-traditional student with three kids, a part-time job, and who hasn't been in a classroom in years, you probably have a common goal: to graduate with the best academic performance possible, having spent the least amount of time studying.

We believe that by using your time well and by studying as efficiently as possible, you'll get more out of your education and you'll have more time for life outside the classroom. A balanced approach to college is a great way to experience the greatest number of learning opportunities, both during and outside of school. We'd like you to be able to take part in as many extracurricular and leisure activities as possible without sacrificing your grades.

We've included the success tools that have proven most beneficial to students in the past, but after you've taken a look through them, you can decide which ones will work for you. As you read through this book, we'd like you to keep one thing in mind: when you are developing your college success skills, you are really developing your employment skills. Our opinion is that there is really only one set of skills that you need in life - a great work ethic supported by a solid system for getting things done - so that in developing 'study skills', you're actually fine-tuning the skills you'll use throughout your career. Well-organized, efficient people are always in demand no matter what the job market conditions; these skills are worth developing.

Now that you've embarked on your education, you may be asking yourself:

have I made the right choice?

Whether you're pursuing a specific profession you've dreamed of since you were 5 years old, or whether you're enrolled in a liberal arts program to explore many different options, it's likely that you've experienced some degree of uncertainty about your career or program choice. You may also feel that now you've made your decision, there's no turning back - and it can be pretty scary to feel you're trapped in a career direction that you're not quite sure of.

Before you spend a lot of time worrying about your future, consider the following: rather than trying to make a final decision right now, approach your career as something that doesn't have to be fully defined at this time. It may be reassuring to know that most people don't have ultimate clarity about their careers. In fact, most of those out in the work force still think about alternative

IN THIS CHAPTER:

- **Choosing your career or program**

- **Employment skills**

- **Career paths**

> "It may be reassuring to know that most people don't have ultimate clarity about their careers."

career paths and opportunities. The bottom line is that there is no perfect or final decision. Careers are always evolving, and it's a rare person who has only one career in his or her lifetime. So it's normal to be in transition, whether you're a first year college student or whether you're a 35 year old sales manager.

As you work toward a particular career, you'll be continually changing, adapting, and revising your career path as you learn about the industry, other opportunities and yourself. As you go through college, you'll be building your knowledge base, making job contacts and developing your work habits. When you get a job, you'll be continually upgrading your skills and keeping abreast of other job opportunities.

What's important is to continually add to your skill base throughout your life, so that you're always prepared for change. People who stay current with trends in the global workplace are better able to find employment opportunities in any economic climate. The most important thing to remember is that it isn't the career you choose that's important - no decision is irreversible or binding - it's the work ethic and attitude you display that will determine your success. If you decide to change your career path, you can always pick up the necessary technical skills if you're willing to invest the time. If, for example, you are studying to be an accountant, the skills you are developing are transferrable to other careers. And if after 10 years you decide you've had enough of the numbers game, you have other options. You can use what you've learned as an accountant in the next career you choose. Because you understand finance and you've had a chance to observe many people's business operations, you may decide you'd like to run your own business. The business management expertise you've picked up as an accountant will have prepared you well. Moreover, if you consistently focus on developing the skills that are universal to any profession, you'll always be employable, and employable people always seem to have career options.

So don't sweat it if you haven't resolved the career issue. Many people spend too much energy deliberating and analyzing their future. They want to know exactly where they're going, but where they are going will probably change many times before they get there. And no one ever really 'gets there', at least not permanently, so relax, and focus on developing the one thing that is certain you'll need: employment skills.

help wanted

What are the most important things managers look for in their employees? The universal employment skills we've talked about have four components: positive attitude, work ethic, commitment to quality, and willingness to learn.

Positive attitude: Employers seek this kind of person for a number of reasons. Since you will be representing your company every time you are in contact with another person, it is essential that you come across positively. Your company's image will be enhanced each time you deal with a customer in a professional, positive manner.

Companies are also are looking for people who view problems as challenges and setbacks as opportunities for growth. A positive frame of mind is a conscious decision that you can control. For example, you can make the choice of seeing your classes as a necessary evil or a stepping stone to your future.

Work Ethic: This means being committed to doing whatever it takes to get a job done. It means seeing the job through to completion, regardless of the obstacles. It means working hard. And it sometimes means digging down deeper than you think you can to finish the job off.

Commitment to Quality: This is caring to do it right, from the smallest job to the biggest project. As a consumer, you probably expect outstanding customer service and product quality when you make a purchase. How does this relate to you? If excellence is demanded by employers, it's essential to develop and implement excellence in all you do. For example, if you work part-time and you're faced with a tedious chore, think about your task from the owner's perspective, as if they were your dollars invested in the company. This mindset may help you see the value in seemingly meaningless jobs. It's doing the small things right that make a company and/or an individual successful.

Similarly, if you've got a college assignment to do, work on it as if you're preparing a proposal for your employer, or as if you are being evaluated for a job based on the quality of the assignment. Few people would send their boss a hand-written memo full of spelling errors, but some students don't think twice about handing in an assignment of similar quality. If you set employment standards for your college work, you'll develop a habit of producing quality work.

Willingness to Learn: Learn to welcome unfamiliar situations, to look upon them as learning opportunities. If a situation requires you to learn a new skill or take a professional development course, do it with enthusiasm. Be willing to upgrade your skills, whether at night school, workshops, or industry conferences. The more you learn, the more valuable you are as a company resource, and the more well-rounded you are as a person.

If you keep these concepts in mind as you're making your way through college, they'll become second nature to you. You'll be developing a professionalism that will see you through your career, and you'll have a head start on everyone else entering the job market.

the ideal candidate

There are some other ways you can make yourself more employable. The following attributes will help you find a job upon graduation.

Group Skills: One of the most important aspects of any job is the ability to work well in a group. Few people work in isolation, so it is essential that you be able to deal effectively with all personality types in groups of all sizes. Not only will your value as an employee be increased because you can cope in any

"Few people would send their boss a hand-written memo full of spelling errors, but some students don't think twice about handing in an assignment of similar quality."

"Your road to a career starts now and will continue as long as you are in the work force."

situation, but you'll experience less of the personal frustration that often accompanies personality conflicts. Leadership and communication skills are also a part of group dynamics.

Problem Solving Skills: It is important to be able to think critically, evaluate situations, collect information, and produce solutions independently.

Computer Skills: It's a rare job that doesn't involve at least some computer work. You can greatly enhance your skill portfolio by learning as many different software programs and operating systems as you can. In fact, many job candidates are selected because of their computer skills.

Networking: Many students graduate believing that their degree or diploma will automatically get them a job within their field. However, finding a job also takes a lot of ground work. It's been said that 85% of all jobs aren't advertised, so it's the people with the right contacts who are ultimately successful in getting these jobs. The old saying "It's not what you know, it's who you know" has more than a measure of truth to it.

Creating contacts within your industry should start now and continue throughout college. Networking could involve your classmates, your faculty and any contacts they may have, your career resource center, professional associations, conferences and events, and information interviews with professionals within your industry.

Work Experience: Since employers are looking for someone with experience, your work history is arguably the most important component of your resume. To gain relevant work experience, you can either volunteer your time, or work part time in your field. A part time job may be more appealing, since you get paid for your efforts. However, jobs can be scarce, and many students don't have time to commit to regular hours. Volunteer work is an ideal way to gain valuable experience, and is no less valid an experience than work you get paid for. Find out which events or conferences are being held within your chosen field, and volunteer your time at as many of these as you can. You could also approach a company you'd like to work for and offer your services to them. When you're ready to look for full time employment, you'll have more to add to the work experience section of your resume. Moreover, a part time job and/or volunteer work can often be that 'foot in the door' that leads to a full time job.

Your road to a career starts now and will continue for as long as you are in the work force. It's the people who continually look for ways to learn, develop, research, network and enjoy that generally have the smoothest career paths. All the best in yours.

timing*is*everything

2

Do your work. It's as simple as that. Complete assignments on time, study for your tests, and do your homework. That's the secret of time management - getting your work done. The difference between knowing about commitments, and actually getting around to doing them is the difference between a poor time manager and a good one. And the secret of a great time manager is someone who gets work done early, so that they've got time to do a quality job.

We believe that if, at the very least, you keep up with your assigned work, you'll probably make it through successfully. Why? It seems that once the work piles up and you get too far behind, it's almost impossible to catch up. In fact, unsuccessful students pinpoint falling behind as the largest contributing factor to their failure.

The advantages to staying ahead of your workload are many: you enjoy your work more, you learn more, you don't get stressed out, you have time for quality, you get better grades, your overall college experience is more fulfilling. Many people use schedules to help them with their balancing act.

staying on top of it all

It may sound obvious, but keeping track of what you have to do ensures that you don't forget to study for a test or keep a commitment. We recommend using schedules to give you a visual picture of how much work is building up. This will help you spread out your workload, so you'll be less likely to hit a crunch time and have to pull all-nighters to get everything done. Three different types of schedules will help you stay on top of it all.

semester schedules

A calendar that displays one semester at a time will allow you to keep track of important dates and deadlines. If you keep your semester schedule out where you can see it, you'll always be aware of what's upcoming, so you can plan how and where to spend your time. We've included a semester and weekly schedule at the back of the book for your use.

weekly schedules

This type of schedule will give you a detailed picture of your week's activities. Start by filling in your 'must do's' - classes, study hours, and then leisure time.

Regular Study Hours?!
Scheduling regular study periods is a practice that is foreign to most students. While we acknowledge that there are more exciting things to do than study, we can offer three reasons why you may consider giving it a try.

1. Practice makes perfect.
Think back to when you were first learning your multiplication tables. Your

IN THIS CHAPTER:

- **Time management and scheduling**

- **Proven time management techniques**

- **Students with part-time jobs**

- **Mature students**

elementary school teacher probably had the whole class recite each times table until you had them memorized. Repetition and review are two core principles of learning; the more you practice, the faster and better you learn. Study periods give you the opportunity to look over your notes regularly, so that studying for a test is a quick review, not a monumental task.

2. Get more done.
Most students limit their study time to completing homework assignments. We're not knocking that - it's certainly important to do your homework. But on a light homework day, you could get a lot more done. Let's say you've set aside 2 hours to study on a given evening, and your homework only takes 45 minutes. You could use the remaining hour and 15 minutes to work on a major report or to review the day's notes. Your workload later in the semester will be lighter, when you'll probably need and appreciate the extra time.

3. Become a more efficient learner.
It's been proven that if you study at the same time in the same place on regular days, you become conditioned to study. In other words, when you sit down at your desk and open your books, your brain knows what you're there for. You don't have to sit around for 20 minutes trying to get into the right frame of mind. It becomes automatic.

Be Realistic
However you decide to schedule your time, be realistic about yourself. If you know you're not going to sit down for 4 hours every Tuesday night and study, don't schedule it. Far better to set aside 2 hours and follow it through. And if you can't live without watching your favorite weekly sports telecast, don't try to make yourself study then. A schedule is only effective if it suits your individual personality.

daily schedules
A 'to do' list will remind you of what you have to do each day. Prioritize each item on your list, labelling the most important items 'A', the less important ones 'B', and the 'nice to do' items 'C'. Start with your A's so that you finish your most important tasks first, and then work through your B's and C's.

time wise
Scheduling can help you manage your time, but there are other ways of getting the most out of a day. We've compiled a list of time management techniques that have proven useful to other students.

1. Do it now.
It's a simple concept, but if you decide to tackle one of the items on your 'to do' list right now, your list will disappear before you know it.

2. Say no.
There's nothing more tempting than an invitation to go out with a group of friends, and sometimes you really need a break from your books. However, if

Mike's 'To Do' List - Wednesday

A   Proofread essay before
     handing in
B   Read Chpt. 4 of accounting
     text
A   Study for mgt. test
C   Call Sue
A   Return library books
A   Mgt. homework assignment
C   Wash dishes
B   Do laundry
A   Call home
C   Buy computer disks at
     bookstore
A   Book racquetball court
     (1:45 p.m.)

you can put a higher priority on studying for a term test, for example, the results will be worth the effort. If you can't say no, see if you can't force yourself to fit in your study period before you go out.

3. Use your class time well.
Attend. There's no real substitute for being there. Information is better retained if you hear it firsthand. When it's time to study for a test, you'll remember more than if you had copied someone's notes (and you'll be taking the chance that his notes are complete and easy to understand). Your study time should therefore be shorter and easier. **Listen carefully.** The more you absorb in class, the less you have to relearn on your own. **Take notes.** If you keep a good set of notes, studying for tests and exams will be easier.

4. Start projects as soon as they are assigned.
Many people have the best of intentions, but few ever follow through on this concept. It's probably one of the most important, though, since the reason for most D papers is the fact that they were written the night before they were due. Assignments always seem to pile up, and you may find that 3 or 4 major papers are due at the same time. A little work on a report every week will allow you time to add quality to your work.

5. Divide each task into small, manageable chunks.
When school work piles up, it's often hard to know where to start. Sometimes it seems as if you'll never get everything done. Break each task into smaller parts, and the work won't seem as overwhelming. For example, instead of facing a whole chapter of your business administration text, set a goal of reading 8 pages.

6. Use small pockets of time well.
Many students feel it's not worth doing school work between classes because they won't have time to complete it. If you've broken your homework and assignments into smaller chunks, though, you'll be able to complete one or two of them in that time. You may even find yourself with a free evening.

7. Use your best time well.
Some people are 'morning' people, so they should do as much work as possible early in the day. Nighthawks are better to save their work until the evening, when they are most effective.

8. Don't put off until tomorrow what you can do today.
Before the day is over, do one more thing that you were saving for 'tomorrow'. In time, you'll find that you aren't procrastinating as much. Moreover, your workload will be lighter.

9. Turn off the television.
*M*A*S*H* reruns are a great way to relax, but when you add *Oprah Winfrey*, *Wheel of Fortune*, and *America's Funniest Home Videos* to the list, you may look back at your day and wonder where it's gone. Unless it's a 'can't miss' show, try to save television until you've finished your homework.

10. Try the ten minute ticker.
If you've got a 'to do' on your list that you find particularly unpleasant, try

"The reason for most D papers is the fact that they were written the night before they were due...A little work on a report every week will allow you time to add quality to your work."

working hard on it for 10 minutes. You may find you don't mind continuing beyond the 10 minutes; at the very least, you'll have more of it done.

11. Stop studying.
Some people get carried away with trying to do too much. Make sure that your studies don't take over your whole life. It's important to balance a variety of leisure activities with college work.

> "Make sure that your studies don't take over your whole life. It's important to balance a variety of leisure activities with college work."

students with part time jobs

Balancing school, homework and your personal life takes careful time management. When you take on a part-time job as well, it can be a challenge not to burn out. If money isn't a survival issue, try to limit your work hours. It's tough to be effective at anything when you're exhausted. However, if your job is essential to your finances, you may want to consider the following:

1. Don't waste your time.
You probably won't have much free time, so it will be important to use every minute well. If you've got a free hour between classes, try to get as much homework done as possible. If you finish lunch early, you could read a chapter of your text.

2. Don't try to stick to a set schedule.
Many students find it more effective to keep a 'to do' list, and then use each pocket of free time in their day to complete each item, in order of priority.

3. Take care of yourself.
You can't afford to let yourself get run down, so eat well and try to get as much rest as you can.

non-traditional students

If you're a non-traditional student, you face an added number of concerns. Will I fit in? Am I too old? Will I remember how to write an exam? How will I handle school and a family?

What's important for you to remember is that you've developed time management and organizational skills during your working years and while raising your family. These skills will help you manage your life during your college years. Faculty and administration are aware of your additional responsibilities, and are supportive of the individual needs you may have.

Non-traditional students generally do well because they have a clear purpose for attending college - a change in career, for example - so they are motivated and committed to their studies. The downside to this is that they often strive for excellence, placing yet another demand on themselves. Considering family, financial, and academic pressures, it's important to realize that you can't do it all. It's okay to be satisfied with 'good enough'.

notetaking

3

"Do I need to write this down?"

How many times have you asked yourself this question in the middle of a lecture? Deciding what's important enough to include in your notes and what's not can be difficult and frustrating. Teachers tell you that you shouldn't try to write down everything that's said in class, but you don't want to leave out important information. On top of that, it's often hard to keep up with the pace of the lecture, and key points can slide by before you get them down. The system of notetaking that we endorse helps to eliminate these difficulties by simplifying the process to a single question: Is this likely to be on a test or exam? In other words, you write down only the concepts and ideas you feel you will be tested on, in a format that simultaneously prepares your study notes. This system is called 4R, and is comprised of good listening skills and selective notetaking skills.

listen to this!

To be an effective notetaker, you have to be a good listener. It's tough to keep your mind from wandering during a class, but you'll save yourself a lot of aggravation if you can stay tuned in to the lecture. First of all, you won't miss the important stuff, so your notes should be complete. You won't have to spend time copying a classmate's notes to supplement your own. Secondly, studying for a test should be easier. When you really listen to a lesson, you'll be surprised at how much of it you remember when you go back to review your notes. You'll be refreshing your memory rather than looking at the material for the first time. We've got some tips on how to "LISTEN" to even the driest subject matter.

L- Lead

Keep yourself in the lead; prepare for your classes. **Prepare physically** - Be ready to write as soon as your professor starts talking. Often an outline of the lecture is given at the beginning of the class, so you can make note of the key areas of importance. **Prepare mentally** - a few minutes spent preparing for class is time well spent. Skimming the next chapter of your text to become acquainted with new vocabulary and ideas will make the lecture easier to follow. This will help you decide what's important and what's filler. A quick glance at your notes from the previous class will refresh your memory and set the stage for the present class. This review is especially helpful for students who are having difficulty.

I - Ideas

If you try to write down everything that's said in a lecture, you end up listening word by word rather than listening for the meaning of what's being said. Instead, try to look for the main ideas and concepts that should be included in your notes.

S - Summarize

As you listen, try to summarize the lecture into key concepts and ideas. Your professor will indicate main ideas by using phrases such as "in conclusion...", "four reasons for...", "the characteristics of ...". When you hear these kinds of cue words, it's a good idea to include the information in your notes.

T - Talk

Take part in the class. Even if you don't like a particular subject, you might as well try to make the best of it. You've got to be there anyway, and you may find that you enjoy the class more if you take on an active role. Answering questions and offering relevant opinions can turn a class into an interesting discussion, and help you resist daydreaming.

When you're having trouble grasping a particular concept, don't be afraid to ask for clarification. If you're afraid you'll look stupid, look at it this way: it's better than trying to teach yourself something you don't understand when you're studying for a test.

E - End

The last five minutes of the class is often a summation of the lecture. Use this time to fill any holes in your notes, rather than packing up your books so you can be the first one out of the classroom. The conclusion is a valuable part of the lesson.

N- Notes

Take good notes. Listening effectively is the first step of notetaking, but you'll retain as little as 20% of the lecture after only 24 hours unless you review. We've got some ideas on how to keep your notes to a minimum, yet contain the maximum amount of information.

> "The first class of each course lays the foundation for the rest of the semester, so it's important to be there."

first class notes

Before we go into the specific details of notetaking, we would like to make a case for getting off to a good start. The first class of each course lays the foundation for the rest of the semester, so it's important to be there. Course outlines are introduced, teacher expectations detailed, and marking systems explained. This ground work will help you tailor your style of notetaking to your instructor's teaching style. Does she lecture straight from the text? If so, you may simply have to highlight key passages of your textbook. Are her lecture notes a supplement to the text? Or does she not use a text? If this is the case, your notes will have to be much more detailed. Whatever your professor's style of lecturing, you'll need a notetaking style of your own.

taking notes in class

The method of notetaking we recommend is the 4R method. It's a simple system that will save you an enormous amount of study time, because the notes you take in class are your review notes. Before you begin, divide your page into two columns by drawing a vertical line on your page about 2 1/2" from the left edge. Some bookstores carry 4R notepaper (also called Cornell paper) to save you the bother of drawing the lines yourself. The 4 R's are explained below.

Recall/Summary	Main Column
1. Record.	During the lecture, record in this column the most important facts and ideas presented.
2. Reduce.	As soon after the lecture as possible, review your notes to see if they make logical sense, and then summarize (reduce) the facts into key words and phrases in the recall column. Write in questions you think you may be asked on an exam. These key words will act as test questions when you study. Note areas that need clarification.
3. Recall.	Cover the main column. Using only your cues and questions, see how much of the content you can recall *aloud*. Then uncover your notes to see how accurate you were. This procedure is extremely effective in transferring facts into your long term memory. It's the same way actors learn their lines.
4. Review.	If you review your notes regularly, you'll retain most of the information. Studying for an exam will then be a review process, not a learning process.

"If you review your notes regularly, studying for an exam will be a review process, not a learning process."

The 4R system will definitely help you study more effectively, but what if you need help deciding what's important enough to write down? What if you can't keep up with your teacher? How can you best organize your notebooks?

notetaking tips

If you look at tests and exams as a summary of your courses, and your notes as the answers to test and exam questions, you'll have an easier time pinpointing what you should include in your notes. Here are some other ideas:

1. Read/skim your text before class.
We've mentioned this briefly, but we'd like to emphasize three benefits:
i) When the lecture begins, you'll know which are the main areas of study, and which are less important.
ii) You'll be more familiar with the terminology/vocabulary.
iii) The lecture will be reinforcement; you'll be getting your first review of the topic when everyone else will be hearing it for the first time.

> "The first five minutes of a class is usually a summary of the previous class...the last five minutes is either a summary of the lesson, or is packed with everything your instructor couldn't fit into the first 45 minutes."

2. Go early, stay late.

The first five minutes of a class is usually a summary of the previous class. Getting there early and setting up before your teacher begins will allow you several minutes to go over your notes. You'll be ready to add anything you've missed. If your instructor gives an outline of the upcoming lesson, you'll be able to jot it down.

You can count on a busy end to the class. The last five minutes is either a summary of the lesson, or is packed with everything your instructor couldn't fit into the first 45 minutes. If you put away your books early, you could be missing the most important part of the lecture.

3. Sit close to the teacher.

A correlation exists between grades and where you sit in the classroom. There are exceptions to the rule, of course, but generally, the closer to the front of the room a student sits, the higher the marks she earns. Why?

Sitting up front makes it easier to keep your attention on the lesson, as there are fewer distractions. It's easier to hear your professor. And it seems that students who sit near the instructor work harder.

4. Don't try to take down everything.

It's impossible, and you'll only get frustrated. Focus on the main points and any examples used to illustrate them. Important ideas are indicated by:
i) time - the more time spent on an idea, the more important the idea.
ii) blackboard/overhead - if it's written on the board or shown on an overhead, it's probably important.
iii) videos, films - if your teacher takes the time to show you a video on the subject, you'll know it's a significant area of study.
iv) emphasis - if the concept is repeated many times, it's another indication of key material.
v) teacher - if she looks at her notes carefully before making a point, it's likely to be important.
vi) summary statements - they often contain the concept in capsule form.

5. Use abbrev.

Your own set of abbreviations and symbols will save you time in class. We have a list of examples, but we emphasize that whichever you use be familiar to you. It won't do you any good to make up a whole new system and then forget what the symbols mean when you go back to study your notes.

according to	acc to	important	NB or *
and	&	management	mgt
continued	contd	maximum	max
definition	def	number	#
department	dept	therefore	$\therefore$
each	ea	should be	s/b
equals	=	results in	$\rightarrow$
example	eg	without	w/o
first	1st	versus	vs

6. Use lots of paper.

If you cram your notes together, you'll probably have a tough time deciphering them later on. Use lots of space and they'll be easier to study from. Don't squeeze diagrams or graphs into a 1" square, and label them well so that you'll understand them when you go back to study for a test.

Write on one side of the page only. This is not a waste of paper! Your notes will appear less crowded and will be easier to organize. The left (unused) side of the page can be used for integrating notes from the text, for filling in notes that you've missed, or for making study notes.

7. Leave spaces if you can't keep up.

If your professor is a speed demon, don't panic. Get down what you can, leave spaces, and listen carefully to the rest of the lecture. Immediately after the class fill in the missing information; you should remember most of it. If you don't, borrow a friend's notes to get what you've missed. If you repeatedly have trouble following the lesson, make an appointment with your teacher to talk about possible solutions.

8. Use a separate binder for each subject.

Everyone has her own preference, but most top students prefer this notekeeping system. A small 3-ring binder makes handouts easy to incorporate, and it's easy to insert notes in the right place if you've missed a class. Large binders designed for six subjects fill too quickly. Furthermore, you won't lose your notes for six subjects if you lose one binder.

9. Don't rewrite.

Rewriting your notes as a method of studying is not usually recommended. Reviewing your notes aloud (rehearsing) is faster and more effective reinforcement.

10. Compare notes.

Sit down with two or three classmates and exchange notes; you'll get a different perspective of what the most important course information is. Discussing why your peers took down certain points may help you see what should be included in your notes and what is unimportant.

Taking good notes is essential to your success. Your memory isn't reliable on its own. After only 24 hours, up to 80% of what you absorbed in a lecture is forgotten. Regular review, however, can reverse these numbers so that you retain at least 80% of the course material.

taking notes from your text

Reading some textbooks can be pretty boring. It's tough to keep your mind on the book, and many people find that when they've finished, they can't remember what they've just read.

"The idea is to look for key ideas that are likely to be test or exam questions."

"...try not to get behind. Reading a chapter of your text may seem a great chore on a given evening, but the task takes on monumental proportions when you've got five chapters to plow through."

We'd like to make your reading time a little easier and a lot more productive. We've got a couple of suggestions:

First of all, try not to get behind. Reading a chapter of your text may seem a great chore on a given evening, but the task takes on monumental proportions when you've got five chapters to plow through. And when a task feels too onerous, you may not bother doing it, yet teachers take many of their test and exam questions straight from the text. Short and frequent reading sessions are most effective; it's easier to absorb the material in short sittings.

The textbook notetaking system we advocate is called S4R, and it works along the same lines as the 4R system of classroom notetaking. It's based on the premise that most authors write in outline form, so that each paragraph contains a main idea and supporting details. The idea is to look for key ideas that are likely to be test or exam questions, always keeping in mind that your notes will double as your study notes.

S - Survey
Leaf through the chapter, skimming the introduction, glossary and summary, looking at the review questions, taking note of the titles, subtitles, charts, graphs and illustrations. These will give you a general idea of the chapter's content, and will help you identify the main ideas being presented. The survey should take no more than 5 minutes.

R - Read
As you read the chapter, don't read word by word, sentence by sentence. Rather, skim through unnecessary details, searching only for the main ideas of the chapter. How do you identify them? Generally, they are words highlighted in bold or italics, definitions, and the key concepts you identified in your survey. Remember, you're looking for potential test questions.

R - wRite
Using 4R notepaper (see Taking Notes in Class), write down the important ideas in the main column, and then reduce them to key phrases in the recall/summary column. These phrases will be your review or study questions.

R - Recall
Take a minute to see how much of the content you remember, using your recall phrases as a prompt. Then look at the main column to see how accurate you were. If you go through this process aloud, you'll learn the material far more quickly than if you limit yourself to reading your notes over and over again. Rehearsing your notes aloud may seem far-fetched to some, but we feel that the goal is to learn the material as quickly as you can so that you've got more time for more exciting things. Feeling a little awkward may be worth the end result.

R - Review
Pull out your study notes and review them on a regular basis. Learning is like training for a marathon. It takes lots of training. You wouldn't leave getting in shape for a 26 mile race until the night before; learning and studying require the same preparation.

So that's the S4R method of reading your textbooks. You don't waste time reading unnecessary details, and your study notes are prepared as you read. You focus on grasping only the key concepts, so you don't have to memorize the entire text. When you prepare for a test or exam, it's easy to zero in on what you really need to know. We think the benefits are worth the extra effort.

guidelines for marking your text

If you prefer to make notes directly in your text, make sure that you don't over-mark your book. Too much is worse than not enough - a cluttered book is difficult to read. There are two ways of marking your text: highlighting, and making notes in the margin of the book. Here are some ideas on both systems:

highlighting

If you like to use a highlighter, skim each paragraph before you put any marks on the page. Many times a sentence will seem to be important the first time through, but as you read on, you find that it either isn't as important as you originally thought, or that the same point is made more clearly later on. Once a section is marked, you'll end up studying the information whether it's important or not because it is highlighted. However, if you highlight only 15-20% of your text, you'll save yourself re-reading 80-85% of it at exam time.

marginal notes

If you've chosen to make notes in the margin, use a consistent marking system so that your notes will have some meaning when you start your review. We have a few suggestions:

Underline: <u>key phrases, main ideas</u>

Indicate an important paragraph: }

Make notes in the margin. Some examples are noted below.

def	=	definition
eg	=	example
NB/ *	=	important point
?	=	unclear point
1,2,3	=	items in a list

> "...make sure that you don't over-mark your book. Too much is worse than not enough - a cluttered book is difficult to read."

studyhints*and*shortcuts   4

First year students have a lot of advice about studying thrown at them during the first few weeks of college. "You should study an hour on your own for every hour you spend in class." "Your study habits will have to be a lot different than they were in high school." "You'll have to put in time if you want to get anything out of this course."

Not only is this kind of advice intimidating, it doesn't tell you a lot. What exactly should you be doing during your study time? Does every course require an hour of studying for every classroom hour? And what if you sit down to 'put in time', but find your mind always seems to wander?

Studying isn't as hard as you think. Sure, it takes time and effort, but if you follow a few proven study techniques, you can decrease the amount of time you spend at the books and increase the amount you learn. In fact, we are convinced that study skills play as important a role in college success as intelligence.

17 ways to study smarter

1. Attend classes.
Don't make the mistake of cutting classes and trying to teach yourself from the text. Save yourself the bother - your teacher has already identified the highlights and important points of your textbook for you.

Since it's the information your professor thinks is important that will appear on a test or exam, it makes sense to go to class and find out what that is. You'll then be spending your study time reviewing what you need to know, not teaching yourself what you hope you need to know.

Pay special attention to the last five weeks of the semester. It's been said that 50% of course's work takes place in the last third of the term.

2. Know your instructor.
Take time to learn what's needed to get through each subject. Study the syllabus (course outline) and refer to it periodically to make sure you're on track. Find out your instructor's testing format, grading/marking system and expectations. You'll be able to tailor your work to meet his requirements.

3. Schedule regular study periods.
If you don't set aside a specific time to review, chances are you won't review. The most effective way to learn anything is to rehearse it regularly. Whether you are practicing the piano, sports, or reviewing your notes, you are learning through the principle of repetition.

4. Be realistic.
When you make up your schedule, decide how much time you really want to

study and divide that time among your courses. It's better to spend half an hour on each subject than to plan one hour for each one and not follow through.

5. Establish a regular study area.
When you study in the same place every time, you become conditioned to study there. Your mind will automatically kick into gear, even when you don't feel like studying.

A regular study area also gives you a permanent place to keep your notes, texts, pens and other supplies. You won't waste 10 minutes each day collecting the materials you need - they'll already be there.

6. Study short and often.
Your brain takes in information faster and retains it better if you don't try to overload it. Four short study periods a week are more effective than two long ones for two reasons: (1) frequent repetition is the key to building your memory, and (2) if you leave a long time between study periods, you may forget a good portion of the material you studied.

7. Start study sessions on time.
It sounds like a small detail, but it's amazing how quickly those 10 minute delays add up. Train yourself to use every minute of your scheduled time.

8. Study when you are wide awake.
The majority of people work most efficiently during daylight hours. In most cases, one hour during the day is worth 1 1/2 hours at night. That's one of the reasons we encourage you to use the hours between classes and other small pockets of time during the day wisely.

Decide what your best time is and try to schedule your study time accordingly. You accomplish more when you are alert. If you find yourself nodding off, give in to it. It's better to wake up early to finish the last hour of homework rather than try to get through everything when you can't think straight.

9. Set a specific goal for each subject you study.
You'll accomplish more, faster if you set a specific goal for each study session. Let's say you've set aside 30 minutes to read your accounting text. If you start reading without a particular purpose, you may get only 9 pages read. But if you set a goal of 15 pages in that time period, you'll probably finish all 15.

So instead of sitting down to 'study computer math', you could decide to answer the review questions at the end of the chapter. Or instead of 'studying marketing', you could set a goal of completing the outline for your marketing paper.

One last thing: don't worry if you don't reach your set goal within the allotted time. Either reschedule the task into your next study period or go back to it later that evening if you have enough time.

> "Start assignments as soon as they are given. If you do nothing else from this chapter, do this."

> "When you complete one of the goals you set for yourself, give yourself a reward. It doesn't have to be anything elaborate - a magazine, snack, movie or TV show."

10. Start assignments as soon as they are given.

If you do nothing else from this chapter, do this. A little work on an assignment each week will allow you time to give attention to its quality. Your workload will be spread out, so you'll avoid a log jam near the end of the semester. If your assignment is due near exam time, as many major papers are, you'll avoid using valuable study time completing your paper.

11. Study your most difficult subjects first.

You're most alert when you first sit down to study, so you'll be in the best shape to tackle the tough stuff. You'll also feel better getting the worst out of the way, and you won't be tempted to spend all of your time on easier or favorite subjects.

12. Review your notes regularly.

Taking good notes is the first step; reviewing them regularly is the second. As we keep saying, the best way to learn anything is to review the information (aloud, if you will) often. When the time comes to be tested, you'll only have to review. You won't have to learn it all.

We've outlined a review schedule below. You may want to add to it if you're having difficulty with a particular subject.

1st review:	same day (reduce to key words)
2nd review:	later the same week
3rd review:	1 week later
4th review:	2-3 weeks later
5th review:	monthly

You'll retain up to 80% of the course material in your long term memory.

13. Take regular breaks.

The general rule of thumb is a 10 minute break for every 50 minutes you work. Don't study through your breaks. They rejuvenate you for your next hour of studying.

14. Vary your work.

Try to give yourself some variety in the type of studying you are doing. For example, if you tried to read textbooks for three hours, you'd not only get bored, you'd have trouble processing the information. Instead, alternate reading, taking notes, doing homework, and writing papers. It's important to vary the subjects you're working on, too. A change is as good as a rest.

15. Problem solve.

For courses that require you to solve problems, such as math, physics, chemistry and statistics, spend a good portion of your study time working on problems. Much of the testing content will be presented in problem form, so you'll be preparing yourself for exam time. If you get stuck on a homework question, don't spend the rest of the night on it. Go on to the next question and ask for help the next day.

16. Reward yourself.

When you complete one of the goals you set for yourself, give yourself a reward. It doesn't have to be anything elaborate - a magazine, snack, movie or

TV show. The reward system gives you an incentive to reach your goals, and a pat on the back for achieving them.

17. Keep on top of it.

Letting work pile up can leave you with an overwhelming task. It's easy to feel that you'll never get on top of it again. If you find yourself falling behind, you may need to improve your study skills. Maybe your time management skills need some work. Or maybe the solution is as simple as cutting down on your social time. Identify the problem as soon as you can, and don't let it become unmanageable.

I can't concentrate

If you're the kind of person who sits down to study and ends up daydreaming about where you're going Saturday night, you might find the following concentration techniques helpful.

Clear your mind.

When thoughts of things to do jump into your head, free your mind by dealing with them right away. If a particular job won't take long to do, you may want to get it out of the way right now. An alternative is to jot it down on your 'to do' list for later.

Focus!

Mental discipline works. If you tell yourself "I'm going to study hard for this exam, and when I'm finished I can daydream all I want", you'll find that you're better able to keep your mind on your work. It's been proven that you can train yourself to develop your concentration abilities.

Don't worry about it.

Try not to spend your study time worrying about personal problems. It's easier to say than do, but try to put your problems aside while you're working. If they continue to dominate your thoughts, don't try to study. You simply won't be able to get anything done. Give them your full attention and try to come up with solutions. If things get too bad, talk to a friend, teacher, or make an appointment to see a college counselor.

Switch subjects frequently.

If your attention span is short and you are easily bored, switch the subjects you are studying frequently. Variety helps ward off boredom.

Do not disturb.

Shut yourself away from noise and other distractions. Don't give yourself a chance to be diverted. Television, phone calls (have someone take a message), family commotion and nearby conversations will all hamper your concentration.

Zzzzzzzzzzzzzz.

Lack of sleep destroys your ability to concentrate. Most people need between 7-9 hours of sleep every night. Your body functions best on a schedule;

"Mental discipline works...It's been proven that you can train yourself to develop your concentration abilities."

constant changes in your sleep habits are both physically and mentally disruptive.

Close the curtains.
Your study area shouldn't look like a prison cell, but windows and posters invite your attention. The less your surroundings distract you, the better you'll be able to concentrate.

don't forget to remember

If you weren't lucky enough to be born with a photographic memory, you can improve your ability to retain information by following some of the memory techniques outlined below.

Be Selective
Pare down the information to the key facts - you'll have less to remember. With practice you'll learn to take down only what is important.

Repeat After Me
Repetition is the key to a good memory. The fastest and surest way to transfer information from your short term to your long term memory is to rehearse or review often, preferably aloud. If you've ever had to recite a poem or book passage in front of an audience, you probably practiced aloud until you had it memorized. It's an effective way to learn.

Intend to Remember
If you decide to remember the material, you will. If this sounds too simplistic, think about how a waiter makes a conscious decision to remember your order. He remembers it because he has to. By the same token, if you make a commitment to remember your course material, you will.

Like What you Learn
When you're interested in something, the details are easier to remember. A baseball fanatic, for example, can remember ERAs and batting averages without any difficulty. The same person may have a terrible time remembering scientific formulas, especially if he doesn't like the subject. If you can turn the material into a personal interest, it will be easier to retain. It may help to see the course as part of a long term career goal.

Find Meaning in It
Information that is meaningful is learned more quickly and remembered longer. When you are trying to learn something that you don't understand or is unrelated to anything you know, it's very difficult to retain. If you can associate it with something you're familiar with, you'll have a much easier time committing it to memory.

Get Organized
Sometimes categorizing the material will make it more meaningful. You might have a hard time remembering your shopping list in the first formation, but when you rearrange the items into categories it suddenly becomes a much easier task.

"Repetition is the key to a good memory."

pens	laundry detergent	paper
shampoo	Kraft dinner	peanut butter
bread	binders	paper towel

School	Food	Household
pens	Kraft dinner	laundry detergent
paper	peanut butter	shampoo
binders	bread	paper towel

Find a Pattern

Learning miscellaneous items or lists can be difficult unless you find a pattern to help you remember them. If you had to remember the number 16385, for example, you could break it into two patterns:

1-3-5 (odd)

6-8 (even)

Rhymes

"In 1492, Columbus sailed the ocean blue."

"Thirty days hath September, April, June and November."

Few of us ever forget rhymes. You might want to try your hand at rhyme to help you remember small details or major concepts.

Acronyms

SCUBA (<u>S</u>elf-<u>C</u>ontained <u>U</u>nderwater <u>B</u>reathing <u>A</u>paratus) is a well-known acronym. HOMES reminds you of the names of the Great Lakes (<u>H</u>uron, <u>O</u>ntario, <u>M</u>ichigan, <u>E</u>rie, <u>S</u>uperior).

Both rhymes and acronyms can be effective memory tools, but only if you don't spend all of your study time trying to devise them.

Assign a Number

If you were trying to remember the types of joints in the human body, it would help to jog your memory if you knew that there were five kinds. In a test situation, if you could remember only four types but knew that there were five, you would be more likely to come up with the fifth type.

Come to Your Senses

Hearing and sight play important roles in memory work. That's one of the reasons we promote rehearsing (hearing) notes. Imagine how hard it would be for a comic to learn his routine without practicing it aloud. Rehearsing also makes it easier to detect any errors or weak areas, and moves facts from your short term to your long term memory faster.

Sight (visualizing) gives your mind a picture to associate with the information. Visualizing actual events, diagrams and illustrations, or important points marked with colored pens, will paint you a mental picture that will help impress the material into your memory.

Keep it Short

Study periods can last up to 50 minutes if you're reviewing, taking notes or doing homework, but for straight memory work they shouldn't be longer than

"When you're interested in something, the details are easier to remember."

20-30 minutes without a break.

Concentrate on the Middle
The material you review at the beginning and end of your study sessions will be remembered best, so you won't need to spend as much time on it as you will the middle content.

Sleep on It
If you review your notes right before you go to bed (assuming you're still alert), your brain will continue to process the information all night, reinforcing it as you sleep. It's an easy way to learn!

read between the lines

As much as 85% of your college work involves reading. It follows, then, that the better you read, the more success you'll have in your courses. If you find reading an effort, don't worry. Comprehension and speed can be improved with practice. Daily practice is most effective, and only fifteen minutes a day will do it.

Choose something you find easy to comprehend and read it at your best speed. Take note of how much material you got through after 15 minutes, and take a second to make sure you absorbed the important details (if you didn't, you were probably reading too quickly). For the first two weeks, continue to read the same type of material and see how many more pages you can read in each fifteen minute period. Push yourself a little, but don't compromise on comprehension. Keep a record of your progress.

Gradually increase the difficulty of your reading material, and follow the same procedure as above. In six weeks or so, you'll have greatly improved your reading ability.

studying isn't everything

There's more to college success than studying. Your relationship with your teachers, your attitude and your involvement in college life can all make your college years more enjoyable and productive.

your faculty

It's important to get along with your faculty. Often a dislike for a teacher results in a dislike for the subject, which in turn, can result in a lower mark. The question isn't "Do I like this teacher?", but rather "How much can I learn from this teacher?" A good relationship with your faculty will maximize your learning experience.

"College doesn't begin and end in the classroom. Getting involved in college life will give you a well-rounded education."

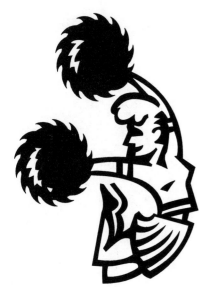

the right approach

Learning and studying require dedication and commitment. So does playing varsity basketball. The connection? They're both hard work, as are most things, but it's how you approach them that makes them enjoyable or a drag. The same intensity for basketball can be put into your school work, with similar results: personal satisfaction from your efforts.

It's easy to maintain a positive attitude about your studies if you surround yourself with people who want to get the most out of their college education. Instead of putting continual pressure on you to go out for a good time, they'll have more interest in getting their homework done, and will encourage you to do the same.

college life

College doesn't begin and end in the classroom. Getting involved in college life will give you a well-rounded education. Movie nights, intramurals, public lectures, student council, interest clubs, the library and the athletic complex will add to your enjoyment of college.

papers*reports*assignments 5

It's essential to develop good writing skills, since most jobs will require you to turn out effective business communications. Your papers and assignments will give you a foundation for writing business memos, letters and proposals.

Keep it Simple
Many people try to add quality to their papers by using big words and complicated sentence structure. However, these often have the opposite effect. A concise writing style is easier to read and understand. Simple words are generally most effective. A thesaurus is a great writing aid, and will help you select the most precise words for your thoughts.

Sentences cluttered with unnecessary words are also confusing to the reader. "I myself" is commonly used but is incorrect; "I" alone is all you need. Other phrases such as "due to the fact that" ("because" will do), "until such time as" ("until"), and "at this point in time" ("now"), make sentences long and unclear.

Each sentence should include one main idea only, and a paragraph should be comprised of a group of sentences that relate to one common theme.

Do Spelling and Grammar Count?
Nothing puts your credibility in question more than errors in spelling and grammar. Proper punctuation, spelling and sentence structure are essential to your assignment. If your writing skills are weak, you may want to inquire about extra help or peer tutoring. At the very least, be sure to proofread your papers or have someone else read them over before you hand them in; you don't want your teacher focusing on correcting your spelling rather than giving full attention to the content of your report.

IN THIS CHAPTER:

- **Good writing skills**

- **Steps in writing a paper or report**

- **Footnotes and bibliography**

writing your paper or report

Before you begin working on your paper, be sure you understand the precise requirements of the assignment. It's essential that you follow your instructor's directions. Too often students write about their topics from the perspective of the source rather than shaping the material to address their professor's expectations.

the right topic

The first step in writing a good paper is choosing a feasible topic. Poor papers are generally the result of weak topics. Make sure there is enough research and information available to support the topic you've selected.

putting it all together

When you've gathered your research and information, make an outline for your report so that you present the information in logical progression. Write your first draft from your outline, and take a break (preferably for a few days). Then go back and review it for accuracy, content, style, spelling and punctuation. You'll be better able to edit your work when you've been away from it for a while.

begin and end well

The introduction is one of the most important parts of your paper. First impressions count, and you want the person marking your report to consider it an A paper right off the bat. The introduction should give the background of the paper and generate interest in the subject. It should state what the paper will cover: the theme, purpose and scope of the paper.

The conclusion is a summation of the main purpose of the paper, and can include a personal evaluation of the subject and any recommendations you may have.

essays and reports

The format of an essay differs from that of a business report. An essay supports a position through a clear presentation of evidence. Each main point should be presented in its own paragraph in logical sequence. Prove statements with facts, research and illustrations. On the other hand, a business report requires an organized presentation of information.

you can judge a book by its cover

It's important to spend time on the presentation of your assignment. A professional-looking report will often receive a better mark than one that was put together with little thought. Your report folder, title page, table of contents, bibliography, appendices and typewritten or typeset pages will all enhance your assignment and reflect positively on your grade.

footnotes

The proper format for footnoting is outlined below. Your college may have its own set of report writing guidelines, which may include a slightly different format for footnotes and bibliography. Check with your teacher.

For a book:

1. Wilfred Jackson, *Everyday Law* (New York: Harper & Row, 1987), p. 78.

For a magazine:

2. John Hench, "Legal Procedures," *Legal Digest*, May 1989, p. 85.
For additional mentions of a previously noted source:

3. Jackson, p. 98.

> "First impressions count, and you want the person marking your report to consider it an A paper right off the bat."

"A professional-looking report will often receive a better mark than one that was put together with little thought."

bibliography

A bibliography should be laid out in the following format. Keep a list of the resources you use as you conduct your research so that you don't forget to include any. Interviews should also be listed in your bibliography.

Jackson, Wilfred. *Everyday Law*. New York: Harper & Row, 1987.

Hench, John. "Legal Procedures." *Legal Digest*, May 1989, p. 85

plagiarism

Most people think that plagiarizing is copying word for word from a source. However, it also includes taking the thoughts and ideas of others and presenting them as your own. Paraphrasing a source is also classified as plagiarism. Avoid any problems by footnoting properly. Check your college's policy on plagiarism; there are usually severe penalties for those found guilty of an infraction.

how *to* study *for* exams 6

So much emphasis is placed on the importance of exams that just hearing the word can make people nervous. We hope that the following information will make your life during exam week a little easier.

There's no doubt about it - preparing for exams takes a lot of work. We would like to offer our thoughts on how to make your study time easier, more productive and hopefully shorter.

IN THIS CHAPTER:

• **Preparing study notes**

• **Recommended study tips**

• **How to write an exam**

• **Kinds of exams**

• **How to eliminate exam anxiety**

getting started

The first step in preparing for exams is learning the exam format, topics, and the weighting of the exam with regard to your final grade. These details will help you determine what and how long to study. If your instructor won't tell you what's on the exam, pay special attention to her particular areas of interest, and to topics that were emphasized during the semester. If the exam format is objective, you'll need to spend more time learning specific details, while essay exams focus more heavily on general concepts and ideas.

If you used the 4R and S4R systems of notetaking, you'll already have a set of study questions and answers. You won't have to spend time making up study notes. However, if you didn't use these notetaking systems, we've got some suggestions on how to spend the minimum amount of time studying to gain the maximum results.

Probably the best way to start is to prepare a study checklist, similar to a table of contents. Using your notes, text and syllabus, make an outline of the major topics that were covered in the course. Divide each heading into sub-topics. For example, a management student might identify decision-making as a major topic, and identify a sub-topic as the seven steps of decision-making. The checklist should take no more than 15 minutes to prepare, and will provide you with an overview of the entire course. You'll then know what you have to study, and you'll have a good idea how long it will take to cover all the material.

summary sheets

When you've finished your checklist, you'll have a skeleton outline of your course. The next step is to make up a detailed summary sheet for each major topic.

The general idea is to take each sub-topic from your checklist and write down a key word or phrase that will help you remember the entire concept. It is especially helpful to phrase it in question form. For example, a question from the management student's summary sheet might be "What are the 7 steps in decision making?" Information to be included on a summary sheet may include definitions, vocabulary, calculations, any points emphasized in class, a list of items from a paragraph in your text (lists make perfect test questions - beware!).

"What questions would you ask on a test if you were a teacher?"

After you have identified the key word or phrase for a sub-topic, write down all of the relevant information you feel you would need to know for an exam. Do this with each point on your checklist. When you've finished, you'll have a complete set of study notes. You won't have to look at your lecture notes or textbook again. You'll have a neat summary of the entire course in the form of potential exam questions.

A word of caution: write only enough to jog your memory. Don't fall into the trap of rewriting your entire notes. You'll only be wasting time on a lot of details you don't need to know.

how to use your summary sheets

The most effective way to use your summary notes is to ask yourself the questions you've prepared aloud, and to answer them aloud as often as you can.

Rehearsing the answers is the fastest way to learn; reading them over and over is the slowest. Give rehearsing a chance - we're convinced that it won't take you long to see what a difference it makes. You'll learn the material faster. You'll also find out which areas are easy for you and which need a lot of work, so that you can allocate your time accordingly.

practice tests

Practice tests are extremely effective study aids. They work best when you test yourself a few times during the semester, but you'll still benefit if you wait until exam time.

The advantages of practice tests are many: (1) you'll be increasing the number of questions on the exam that will be familiar to you, (2) you'll be giving your study sessions a focus so you'll be less likely to waste time, (3) the best preparation for an exam is to practice exactly what you'll be doing when you actually write it, (4) you'll eliminate the stress of exam time because you'll have answered so many practice questions that the real thing will be old hat to you.

how to set up practice tests

What questions would you ask on a test if you were a teacher?

Keeping this question in mind, set a practice test using your study questions, old exams and textbook review questions. If possible, use the same test format that your professor uses (if that happens to be multiple choice, here's where old exams are particularly helpful).

When you sit down to take the test, simulate test conditions as closely as you can. Whatever you do, don't look at your notes until you've finished the test. You won't get a true picture of what you know and where you need to spend more time.

You can grade your test by comparing your answers to your notes. If you spot an area that needs work, set up the next test to concentrate on that particular topic. Don't spend too much time on the areas you know well.

studying for science and math tests

When you're studying for a math or science exam, start by compiling a summary page of formulas and definitions. Keep details of the steps to follow when solving each particular type of problem, and solve sample questions and problems for each concept.

a grab bag of exam study tips

1. Be prepared.
The most important factor in exam success is preparation. Bar none. No matter how many helpful hints you employ, nothing works as well as making sure you've studied enough.

2. Do your homework.
Often an exam question will parallel a homework assignment. Doing your homework regularly will give you practice where you need it.

3. Review regularly.
If you spend a few minutes each week reviewing your notes, your final studying will be a review, not an attempt to learn the entire term's work.

4. Study your weakest subjects first.
Why? You'll be fresher and therefore better able to deal with difficult areas, and you'll have more time to deal with any problems that arise.

5. Ask for help.
If you're having trouble with a particular subject, don't be afraid to ask for help. Your teacher and fellow students will be glad to give you a hand. Remember, too, that most colleges have peer tutoring programs. See your student services department for details.

However, don't leave asking for help until the last minute. It's impossible to teach a semester of accounting in a week. If you find that you're really struggling with something early on, get help immediately.

6. Understand vs memorize.
You may pass your exams if you memorize the material, but you'll improve your grades considerably if you understand what it is you're memorizing. You'll also find the material easier to remember.

7. Look at old exams.
Some teachers file copies of past exam papers in the library. They can be useful study tools, as long as you don't limit your studying to them.

8. Attend end of semester classes.
A lot of valuable information is outlined in the last few classes of the semester. Points of misunderstanding can be cleared up, exam format explained, and potential exam questions given.

"If you spend a few minutes each week reviewing your notes, your final studying will be a review, not an attempt to learn the entire term's work."

9. Review in a group.

However, make sure the review doesn't take the place of your own study time. Brainstorm possible test questions with your classmates, compare notes, and test each other on the material.

10. Don't study too long.

A 10 hour study marathon will only wear you out. You'll learn more if your study periods are short, frequent and include regular breaks.

11. Eat well and get a good night's sleep.

Take care of yourself during exam week - you're going through a lot of stress. Make sure you hold up well.

"Take care of yourself during exam week - you're going through a lot of stress."

last minute cramming

Although we've included this section on cramming, we don't advise it for one important reason.

Cramming isn't learning. Most of what you cram will be forgotten in 1 or 2 days. In other words, if you cram for a term test, the information won't be there for the final exam. That's why we believe so strongly in regular review. Assuming that you have no other choice, here are the four steps of cramming:

1. Be selective. Don't try to learn everything - it's virtually impossible. Go to your syllabus (course outline), text and notes, and choose a few of the course highlights. Learn these topics as best you can. You're taking a chance on the content of the exam, but you really don't have any other choice. If you try to learn a little about a lot, chances are pretty good you won't remember much of anything.

2. Question and answer. Turn the information you are about to learn into a series of exam questions and answers, and start drilling yourself. Take a five minute break every half hour.

3. Rehearse. Rehearsing the answers aloud is the most effective way of remembering course material. Study as long as you are able, and stop when it seems nothing is sinking in anymore.

4. Do your best. Try to relax, and go out and do the best you can.

how to write an exam

give yourself a good start

The morning of an exam can be fairly stressful. Try to ease the tension by giving yourself a good start to the day.

Get a good night's sleep if you can, and make sure you have a trusty alarm clock. Nothing is worse than writing your exam in a hurried panic because you were late.

Be certain of your exam time and place. Arrive early enough to get settled and arrange your work space, but not too early; it's not a good idea to get into a last minute discussion with frantic classmates. Your friends' worries will only add to your own. And lastly, we don't recommend you sit near your friends. It's too distracting. You'll be tempted to see if you're ahead of or behind their pace, and to make periodic checks as to how they're doing. You'll also be more likely to leave early if you see them walking out ahead of time.

hints for objective exams

Objective exams may include multiple choice, true-false, short answer or matching questions. Nearly all of the information is supplied on the exam itself. In most cases, your job is to recognize the correct answer.

Many students don't study as hard for objective exams, but we encourage you to prepare as well for them as for any other exam. In fact, they are often more difficult than essay exams because there is a definite right or wrong answer. Either you know the correct answer or you don't.

Multiple Choice
Here are some hints to help you with multiple choice exams.

1. Try to answer the question yourself before looking at the answers given.

2. Answer the questions you know first. Mark the ones you're not sure of and go back to them.

3. Your first instinct is usually correct; don't change your answers unless you are sure you made a mistake.

4. Take questions at face value - don't get caught up looking for tricks. There probably aren't any.

5. Watch the meaning of sentences containing double negatives. Cross out both negatives and then answer the question.

If you're having trouble:
6. Rephrase the question in your own words.

7. Underline key words. This can help untangle complicated questions.

8. Look for answers in other test questions.

9. Cross out the answers you know are incorrect, and select your answer from the remaining options.

10. Never leave a question unanswered unless there is a penalty for an incorrrect answer. In that case, answer only if you can narrow your choices down to two.

Take a Guess
No matter how much you study, you're bound to come across at least one question that will have you completely stumped. But even guessing is a science. Here's how to make your best guess:

"Your first instinct is usually correct; don't change your answers unless you are sure you made a mistake."

1. If two answers are similar, choose one of them.

2. If two answers have similar words (perpetrate, perpetuate), choose one of them.

3. If two answers have opposite meanings, choose one of them.

4. Choose the longest answer.

5. If none of the above work for you, choose (b). Studies prove that (b) is the correct answer 40% of the time, (c) is right 30% of the time, (a) 20% and (d) only 10% of the time.

True-False Questions
Since true-false questions are usually worth only 1 mark, don't spend too much time on any one.

1. There are generally more true than false answers.

2. Look for qualifiers (all, most, sometimes, rarely, never). The answer will depend on the qualifier, and more often than not, questions containing qualifiers are true.

3. However, answers that have 'always' or 'never' in them are usually false, since nothing (with the exception of some math and science questions) is true or false 100% of the time.

Short Answer Questions
This is the only kind of objective question that relies on recall, and usually requires a short description or definition.

1. Look for grammatical hints. For example, a sentence that begins with "An_" indicates that the word starts with a vowel.

2. Use the best word or phrase you can think of.

Matching Questions
Take a brief overview of the question before you start, as there are not always an equal number of items to match. Start with the easiest match, and cross out each answer as you use it to minimize the confusion of the question layout.

hints for open book exams
These are often the most difficult exams, because your teacher expects you to answer every question well.

1. Write all formulas, definitions, etc. on a separate sheet of paper for easy referral.

2. Prepare your notes for quick reference. Make a table of contents, number your pages and tab important pages.

"If none of the above (hints) work for you, choose (b). Studies prove that (b) is the correct answer 40% of the time, (c) is right 30% of the time, (a) 20% and (d) only 10% of the time."

hints for science and math questions

1. Translate problems into English to help you understand what is being asked. For example, the formula for calculating interest, $I = P \times R/100 \times T$ would be translated as "Interest equals principal times the rate as a percentage times the time period".

2. Determine the unknown.

3. Determine the known quantities.

4. Write out the formula.

5. Show all your work. Don't skip steps, even if they seem trivial to you. Your teacher needs to see the logic of your answer and may give part credit for each step of the solution.

6. Check for a logical answer. Make sure what you have calculated makes sense.

7. Check to see if you used all of the data supplied. It isn't often that data is given and not used.

8. Proofread your exam. Check the steps of each problem.

hints for essay exams

1. **Read the entire exam first;** roughly estimate the time allowed for each question according to the point value.

2. **Keep the marker happy** - make your exam easy to read. Use pen, double space your answer and write legibly on one side of the page. You don't want your teacher's first glance at your paper to put her into a negative frame of mind.

3. **Answer the easiest question first.** This is a good way to build your confidence. Moreover, a strong first answer will help persuade your teacher that you've prepared well for this exam.

4. **Read the directions carefully,** and do precisely what the question asks you to. If you are asked to compare two theories, you'll lose marks if you explain them, because you haven't answered the question.

A word of caution: one of the most common errors in writing essay exams involves questions with more than one part. If the question reads 'Answer one of the following', don't waste valuable time answering all four parts. Conversely, if it reads 'Answer all four parts', make sure you don't do just three. There is nothing more frustrating than knowing the material, but losing marks because you didn't follow the directions.

5. **Plan your answer.** Make a mini outline, including all of the main points you want to cover. Your outline could be as simple as jotting down points as they occur to you, and then numbering them in the order you want to use them.

"There is nothing more frustrating than knowing the material, but losing marks because you didn't follow the directions."

An outline will allow you to answer the question faster, and you'll be less likely to leave out an important fact. If you run out of time, your teacher will be able to see what you intended to write about, and may give you part credit.

6. Get right to the point. Don't waste time with an introduction. Make your opening statement forceful, and make sure it states exactly what you are going to talk about.

Use your strongest points first to make an immediate impact. You want to convince your professor right off the bat that your answer is worth a high mark.

7. Keep to the point. Write only what is relevant to the question. Remember, marking an essay question is subjective. If the person marking your paper has to wade through pages of filler to find a few good points, she may get annoyed and not mark you as highly as if you used the same points in an organized, compact answer. Most teachers have at least 200 papers to get through, and will look favorably on an exam that is easy to mark. The quality of your answer does not depend on the quantity of words you use.

8. Don't forget to include the basics. You may think that something is too elementary to put down, but it may be the very thing your professor is looking for. She can't assume that you know something you didn't write down, and you may be losing easy marks.

9. Make clear your understanding of the material. Illustrate your answers with examples and diagrams; your teacher is looking for more than memory work.

10. Keep your eye on the time. Make sure you're not spending too much time on one answer at the expense of the others.

11. Always write something. Even if you have no idea how to answer a question, try to relate the answer to other course material, another exam answer, or your general knowledge. At worst you'll get a few marks for your effort.

12. What's the hurry? Don't try to race through the exam. There aren't any marks for finishing first, so you might as well use the time allotted to perfect your paper.

13. Proofread your paper. Have you answered all parts of the question? Make any spelling and grammar corrections, and add any important points you've missed. Pick up as many extra marks as you can.

14. If you run out of time, jot down the last few ideas in point form. Your teacher will be able to see where you were going with your answer, especially if you used an outline before you began.

15. Don't rehash the exam with your classmates afterwards. If you forgot to include something or misinterpreted a question, there's nothing you can do about it now. You'll need all of your energy to concentrate on your next

"Use your strongest points first to make an immediate impact. You want to convince your professor right off the bat that your answer is worth a high mark."

exam, so leave this one behind.

read the directions

You'll come across some of these words when you're writing your exams. Look them over so that you'll understand exactly what each question is asking you to do.

Analyze	Examine in detail. Involves judgment.
Compare	Show similarities and differences.
Contrast	Show differences.
Define	Explain the meaning in a short answer.
Describe	Tell all you know; include as many details as you can.
Discuss	Write everything you know in a logical progression.
Evaluate	Examine the positive and negative aspects, draw a conclusion.
Illustrate	Use specific examples and details.
Justify	Give reasons to support a position.
Outline	Using the main ideas, give an overview.
Prove	Use facts and evidence to support a position.
Summarize	Give the main ideas in a short answer.

relax!

It's easy to say, but a lot more difficult to do when you've got your toughest exam to write and you don't feel you've studied enough.

the abc's of eliminating exam anxiety

A. Think positively. Thoughts such as "I haven't studied enough" and "I don't know the material" will only increase your anxiety level. Instead, try to feel good about what you do know. You hear it all the time, but a positive attitude goes a long way.

B. Take a deep breath. It really will help you calm down. Think of a reward that you'll give yourself when you're through - maybe lunch out or a movie with a friend.

C. If you draw a blank, don't panic. It happens all the time. Take a few minutes to sit back and wait for it to come back to you.

D. Don't look around to see what your classmates are doing. If you're having doubts about how well you're doing and you see someone who looks like they're aceing the exam, it will only add to your anxiety.

E. Prepare well for your exams. People who know the material rarely get nervous. Review regularly and give yourself practice tests.

F. Keep things in perspective.
Although exams are important, they're not a matter of life or death. In later years, nobody will ask you what grades you received on your exams. They lose significance over time.

"Keep things in perspective. Although exams are important, they're not a matter of life or death... They lose significance over time."

managing*college*life 7

IN THIS CHAPTER:

- College survival skills

- Coping skills

- Money and academic concerns

- College services

- Making new friends

college survival skills

Starting college can be difficult. Moving to another city, living on your own, meeting new people, getting used to a new set of academic standards - all of these can present you with quite a challenge. But how you approach a given situation will determine if it gets the better of you, or if you stay on top of it.

It's normal to feel discouraged by a difficult situation. However, things will look a lot brighter if you try to make the best of it. Easier said than done, but how do you turn a negative into a positive?

First of all, try to do something constructive about your circumstances. If you're having a tough time academically, you might talk to a professor about doing an extra assignment to help you pass the course. If a relationship is ending, you could plan a weekend away with a friend.

If there's nothing immediate that you can do, decide how you'll better handle future situations, and try to learn from this experience. Your coping skills will improve with each new experience.

Here are a few qualities that will help you develop your survival skills:

Be Resilient
It's easier to deal with life if you can adapt to any situation. For example, if you can be hardworking and dedicated at exam time, yet be able to leave it all behind when exams are over, you'll be better able to handle whatever you face.

Be Tough
You have to be able to look after yourself. People may hurt you or gossip about you, but it's important to keep their actions from affecting you.

Before you react, though, be certain you are interpreting others' behavior correctly. What you may perceive as a hurtful act may not have been intended as such. Stress can make you blow things out of proportion.

Keep Laughing
A good way to keep a positive outlook is to hold on to your sense of humor. Don't take things too seriously, and you'll be better able to keep things in perspective.

Be Open-Minded
It's easy to be critical of a situation or professor, especially if those around you are doing so. Don't let others be a negative influence on you. Keep an open mind, come to your own conclusions, and you'll enjoy things more fully.

Meet New People
One of the best therapies for depression is to go out and meet new people or

participate in a new activity. You may find that despite your difficulties, there's still a lot out there to enjoy.

Don't Sweat the Small Stuff
A renowned cardiologist's philosophy for dealing with stress: (1) Don't sweat the small stuff. (2) It's all small stuff.

Use the Five Year Rule
Ask yourself: "Five years from now, how important will this problem be?" Nine times out of ten, the answer is "Not very important". The five year rule can keep you from blowing the situation out of proportion.

7 ways to cope with it all
You may find a situation getting the better of you. Here are seven ways to help you cope.

1. Talk to Someone
Don't bottle your problems up. Go to someone you trust and get it off your chest. Sometimes just verbalizing the problem can help you to see it in a different light. If things get bad enough, visit your student services department and set up an appointment with a counselor.

2. Make Your Escape
Taking a break from a difficult situation can do wonders for your frame of mind. Your escape doesn't have to be as elaborate as a vacation; a shopping trip, movie or walk in the park can do the trick.

3. Let it Out
Release your frustration in a productive way; a hard game of racquetball, for example, will ease your tension.

4. Forget About It
Sometimes you've just got to say "This isn't important enough to give my time to", and move on from whatever's got you down.

5. Do Something Nice
If you find you're thinking about your own worries too much, focus on someone else who's dealing with a tough situation. You'll get a good feeling from doing something nice for them, and you'll forget about your own troubles.

6. Do One Thing at a Time
If your work load seems overwhelming, don't get discouraged. Take the most important task that's haunting you and start in on it. Accomplishing even one of your 'to do's' can make you feel like you're back in control.

7. Give Yourself a Break
Some people create stress by setting standards that are too high to reach. Don't try to be perfect - sometimes you'll have to be satisfied with 'good enough'.

"If your work load seems overwhelming, don't get discouraged. Take the most important task that's haunting you and start in on it."

money worries

One of the hardest things you'll do while you're at college is budget your money. When you receive your student loan and you're suddenly 'rich', it can be tempting to run out and celebrate with a shopping spree. Keeping a budget will help ensure that you'll have enough money at the end of the semester. Above all, set a realistic amount for your spending money and stick to it. Spending too much with too little thought is where most students run into trouble. If you see that you are going to run short, you have several options.

A part-time job can bridge the financial gap. Your college's placement office can help you with your job search. You may be eligible for a work study program (see your student services department). The financial aid office offers grant and scholarship programs, and can determine your eligibility for student loans.

In the meantime, we have several ideas to help you stretch your dollars:

Don't carry around a lot of cash. People generally spend as much as they have with them. If you don't have it, you won't spend it.

Put away your credit card. It's easy to overspend, because you don't feel like you're actually paying for the merchandise. It's also easy to forget you've spent the money until the bills come in.

Find affordable rent. If you're living off campus, figure out how much rent you can afford and stick to it. You don't want to have all of your money tied up in housing.

Think again. If you're dying to buy a new CD or pair of jeans, give it some more thought. Often the item won't be as important upon reflection.

Wait until it's on sale. You may save a bundle if you're willing to wait a while.

schoolwork worries

If you don't do as well as you expected on your first few tests and assignments, don't despair. It takes time to become familiar with your professors' expectations and standards.

It's also common to periodically feel snowed under by your workload. Good time management and study skills will help you deal with your anxiety. Whatever you do, don't give up, and don't spend all of your waking hours working. Long work sessions aren't as productive as short ones, and you'll only wear yourself out. Start with one job, and take it one step at a time.

If it all gets too much for you, talk to your teacher(s) to find out where the problem is. Together you can work out a solution.

"If you don't do as well as you expected on your first few tests and assignments, don't despair. It takes time to become familiar with your professors' expectations and standards."

college services

Your college has a number of support services to help you make it through.

Academic Support
. Library, labs
. Peer tutoring program
. Faculty/staff
. Student services
. Registrar's office

College Support
. Career placement office
. Counseling, health services
. Financial aid, housing
. Student Association
. Resident directors, assistants

college friends

Making new friends isn't always easy. Some people meet people more easily than others, but it still takes an effort to form new friendships.

There are two things above all else that will help you make new friends. The first is to simply start a conversation. You have to take the initiative and approach the people you'd like to get to know. Those who sit back and wait for others to come to them may wait a long time.

The second is to be a good listener. People who have a genuine interest in others never seem to lack friends.

It's important to spend time with your friends. Your college experience will be richer for it; some of your best memories of college will be of class parties, intramurals or student activity nights with your classmates.

College is an opportunity to make a fresh start, an opportunity to pursue the goals that are important to you. We wish you all the best in your journey.

"College is an opportunity to make a fresh start, an opportunity to pursue the goals that are important to you. We wish you all the best in your journey."

Semester Schedule

Sunday	Monday	Tuesday	Wednesday	Thursday	Friday	Saturday

Month _____

Sunday	Monday	Tuesday	Wednesday	Thursday	Friday	Saturday

Month _____

Sunday	Monday	Tuesday	Wednesday	Thursday	Friday	Saturday

Month _____

Sunday	Monday	Tuesday	Wednesday	Thursday	Friday	Saturday

Month _____

Weekly Schedule

	Sunday	Monday	Tuesday	Wednesday	Thursday	Friday	Saturday
6:00 am							
7:00 am							
8:00 am							
9:00 am							
10:00 am							
11:00 am							
12:00 pm							
1:00 pm							
2:00 pm							
3:00 pm							
4:00 pm							
5:00 pm							
6:00 pm							
7:00 pm							
8:00 pm							
9:00 pm							
10:00 pm							
11:00 pm							

The Right Start to College

making your mark

About LDF Publishing Inc...

LDF Publishing Inc. has been assisting colleges with student success and retention ideas since 1992. *Making Your Mark* has sold more than 350,000 copies, and is used in over 750 educational institutions across North America. Its strengths are its light and friendly writing style, its comprehensive coverage of essential material, and its cost. We've priced the book so that any college can afford to implement a retention strategy - for as little as $2.25 per copy.

Lisa Fraser, author of *Making Your Mark*, also co-authored *Cornerstone*, the Canadian edition of a student success textbook for Prentice Hall Canada Inc. She has worked as an educational proposal writer, securing funding and grants for college projects, and has taught developmental education classes.

Don Fraser is one of Canada's leading authorities on student success and retention. He has been a professor at Durham College for the past 26 years. He co-designed and implemented Durham's student success program twelve years ago, and has been working in this area since that time. Don has done a great deal of research on student success and retention, and received a NISOD award for his work in this area. He has developed a retention model - The Right Start to College - that has been adopted by many colleges and universities across North America and internationally. Don also co-authored *Cornerstone*, and was a member of the Ontario government's task force on student retention.

Products:

Making Your Mark, ISBN 0-9696427-6-8
Making Your Mark in the OHL, ISBN 0-9696427-7-6
Comment réussir dans ses études, ISBN 0-9696427-3-3
Making Your Mark software for Windows 95

Seminars:

The Right Start to College Seminar
Staff/Faculty Retention Training
KPI Retention Consulting

About Our Products and Services...

Making Your Mark is the foundation of The Right Start to College seminar. We've found that incorporating the book into a first year experience seminar produces dramatic retention results. Workshop outlines are available on our website at:

www.ldfpublishing.com

The Right Start to College workshop has been delivered at the 1998 and 1999 National Conference on Student Retention, the 1999 World Congress of Colleges and Polytechnic, and at individual colleges in New York, Florida, Ohio, Mississippi, Ontario, Manitoba, Quebec, New Brunswick, and Nova Scotia. For more information, or for help in developing your retention program, please contact Don Fraser at (905) 985-9990 or by email at ldf@sympatico.ca.